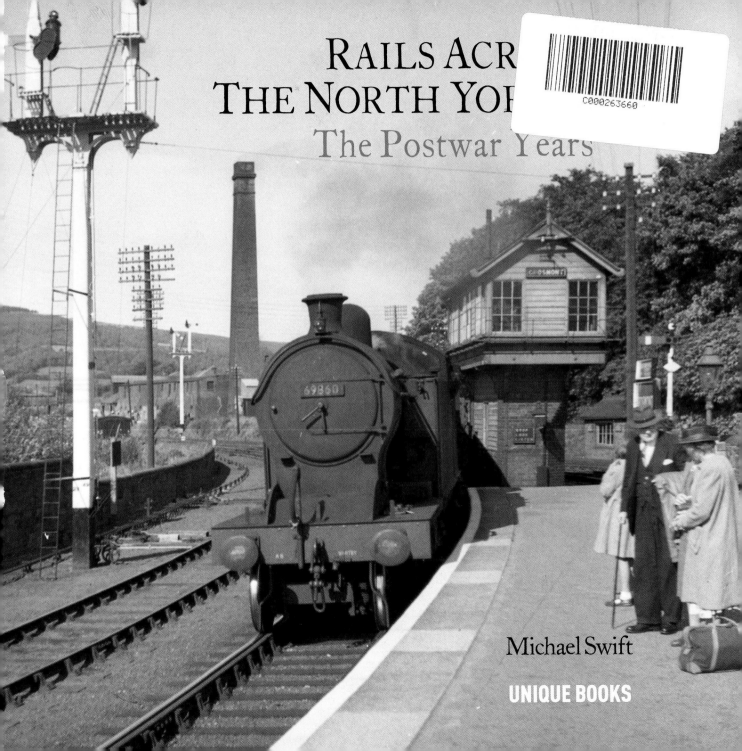

RAILS ACR
THE NORTH YOR
The Postwar Years

Michael Swift

UNIQUE BOOKS

Front cover: With the famous abbey on the hill-top in the background, Thornaby-allocated Class Q6 0-8-0 No 63393 is captured shunting at Whitby. This locomotive, one of a class of 120 built to a design of Vincent Raven between 1913 and 1921, was built at Darlington in October 1918. It was last allocated to Tyne Dock, from where it was withdrawn in June 1964. Sister locomotive No 63395 survives in preservation; now owned by the North Eastern Locomotive Preservation Group, the locomotive is now based on the North Yorkshire Moors Railway.
Neil Davenport/Online Transport Archive

Previous page: As passengers wait on the platform, Class A8 No 69860 approaches Grosmont station from Whitby with a service towards Battersby Junction. Numerically, the largest class of 4-6-2T inherited by the LNER was the 'A8'; this class had originally been completed by the NER as 4-4-4Ts to a design by Vincent Raven and delivered between 1913 and 1922. Designated Class D by the NER and H1 by the LNER, the locomotives had a tendency to roll excessively at high speeds and so all were rebuilt, to a design by Gresley, between 1931 and 1936. The type had originally been planned to operate fast passenger services between Darlington and Newcastle and along the north-east coast. All remained in service until the end of 1956 but then withdrawal was swift, with all being taken out of service by the end of 1960 with No 69860 succumbing in June that year. The NER signalbox in the background closed in 1972, when the line towards Battersby was singled. The box was regarded as unsuitable on safety grounds for use by the preserved railway and was demolished in 1978.
Neil Davenport/Online Transport Archive

Rails across the North York Moors: The Postwar Years

Michael Swift

First published in the United Kingdom by Unique Books 2021

ISBN: 978 1 913555 07 8

A CIP record for this book is available from the British Library

Unique Books is an imprint of Unique Publishing Services Ltd, 3 Merton Court, The Strand, Brighton Marina Village, Brighton BN2 5XY.

www.uniquebooks.pub

Printed in India

A note on the photographs
Many of the illustrations in this book have been drawn from the collection of the Online Transport Archive, a UK-registered charity that was set up to accommodate collections put together by transport enthusiasts who wished to see their precious images secured for the long-term. Further information about the archive can be found at: www.onlinetransportarchive.org or email secretary@onlinetransportarchive.org

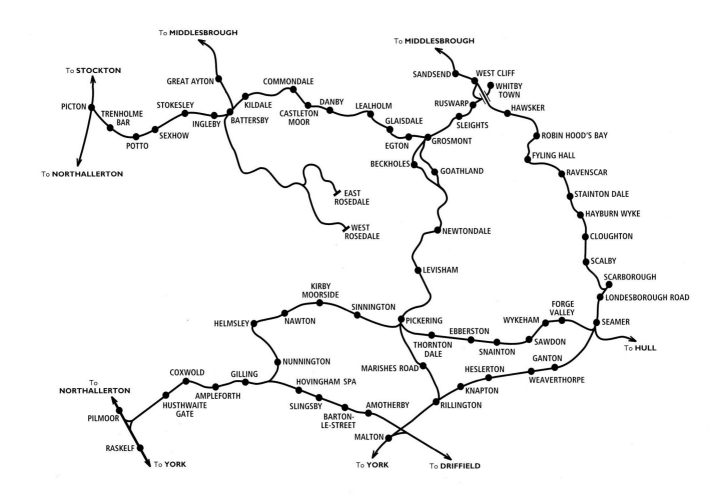

To **MIDDLESBROUGH**

To **STOCKTON**

To **MIDDLESBROUGH**

SANDSEND

WEST CLIFF

WHITBY TOWN

GREAT AYTON

COMMONDALE

PICTON

TRENHOLME BAR

STOKESLEY

KILDALE

DANBY

LEALHOLM

RUSWARP

HAWSKER

POTTO

SEXHOW

INGLEBY

BATTERSBY

CASTLETON MOOR

GLAISDALE

SLEIGHTS

ROBIN HOOD'S BAY

To **NORTHALLERTON**

EGTON

GROSMONT

FYLING HALL

BECKHOLES

GOATHLAND

RAVENSCAR

EAST ROSEDALE

STAINTON DALE

HAYBURN WYKE

WEST ROSEDALE

NEWTONDALE

CLOUGHTON

LEVISHAM

SCALBY

SCARBOROUGH

KIRBY MOORSIDE

LONDESBOROUGH ROAD

HELMSLEY

NAWTON

SINNINGTON

PICKERING

FORGE VALLEY

WYKEHAM

SEAMER

NUNNINGTON

EBBERSTON

THORNTON DALE

SAWDON

To **HULL**

COXWOLD

GILLING

HOVINGHAM SPA

MARISHES ROAD

SNAINTON

GANTON

To **NORTHALLERTON**

AMPLEFORTH

SLINGSBY

AMOTHERBY

HESLERTON

WEAVERTHORPE

HUSTHWAITE GATE

BARTON-LE-STREET

KNAPTON

PILMOOR

RILLINGTON

RASKELF

MALTON

To **YORK**

To **YORK**

To **DRIFFIELD**

3

INTRODUCTION

THE FIRST RAILWAY to serve the area covered by this book was the Whitby & Pickering Railway. First proposed in 1831, the line was authorised by Act on 6 May 1833 and was opened from Whitby to Grosmont on 8 June 1835. The section south, including the rope-worked incline, to Pickering followed on 26 May 1836.

The Whitby & Pickering was taken over by the York & North Midland on 30 June 1845; just over a week later, on 7 July, the York & North Midland section from Rillington Junction to Pickering was opened. The new owner commenced work on the reconstruction of the Whitby & Pickering. Steam operation as far north as Levisham was authorised on 1 September 1846 and the first steam locomotive appeared in Whitby on 4 June 1847. The reconstructed railway, however, continued to use the incline at Goathland for almost a further two decades. Powers to construct the deviation route were obtained by Act on 11 July 1861 and the route opened on 1 July 1865. The York & North Midland became part of the North Eastern Railway on 31 July 1854. The stub from Grosmont to Beckholes of the original alignment regained a passenger service, operated by steam rail-motor in the summer months only, in 1908 and this operated until 21 September 1914; the stub closed to freight traffic on 18 September 1951.

The second railway to enter the region was North Yorkshire & Cleveland; this was authorised on 10 July 1854 to construct a line from Picton to Grosmont to connect with the existing line from Pickering. The line was opened from Picton to Stokesley on 3 March 1857 and thence to Castleton on 1 April 1861; by this date, however, the struggling company had, in July 1858, become part of the NER. Connecting into the new railway at Battersby was the narrow gauge line constructed by the Ingleby Ironstone & Freestone Mining Co; this opened on 6 April 1858 but, following the arrival of the NER, was to be converted to standard gauge from 27 March 1861. The construction of an incline at Ingleby saw this route connected to the Rosedale West branch (opened on 27 March 1861) and that to Rosedale East (opened in August 1865). These lines never carried a timetabled passenger service and their fortunes followed those of the mines served. Following peak production in 1873, production gradually declined until complete closure in 1925; the railway branches finally closed in early 1929.

Having taken over the North Yorkshire & Cleveland, the NER renewed the powers for the construction of the line east from Castleton in an Act of 11 July 1861. The line opened on 2 August 1865.

To the south, the Malton & Driffield Railway was authorised on 26 June 1846; the line opened throughout on 19 May 1853 (official) and 1 June 1853 (public). This was connected to the East Coast main line at Pilmoor courtesy of the Thirsk & Malton Railway (a subsidiary of the York, Newcastle & Berwick Railway); originally authorised on 18 June 1846 but delayed, with construction not commencing until 1 October 1851, this line also opened to the public on 1 June 1853.

The next link in the local network to be completed was the line from Battersby to Nunthorpe which opened, with one intermediate station (at Great Ayton), on 1 April 1868. This was followed by the branch from Gilling to Pickering, which opened opened on 1 April 1875, and by the Forge Valley line, from Pickering to Seamer, on 1 April 1882.

The construction of the line south from Loftus was authorised as the Whitby, Redcar & Middlesbrough Union Railway on 16 July 1866; however, due to the impecunious

Table 110 — MALTON and WHITBY

Miles from Malton		Week Days only								Miles		Week Days only							
		a.m	a.m	a.m	a.m	p.m	p.m					a.m	a.m	a.m	a.m	p.m	p.m		p.m
				C	S	C								C	S				
103	Newcastle .... dep	2 1	..	8 15	10 0	1F 42	V30	..		—	Whitby .... dep	7 5	7 48	9 30	1145	3 20	..		6 45
116	Leeds (City) .. ″	3 0	..	9A10	12P 5	1R50	4 0	..		1½	Ruswarp	7 10	7 53	9 35	1150	3 25	..		6 51
109	York .... ″	4 30	..	10J15	1 20	3K 55	8	..		3	Sleights	7 14	7 57	9 39	1154	3 29	..		6 55
—	Malton .... dep	5 20	..	11 5	2 3	4 0	6 0	..		6¼	Grosmont	7 23	8 6	9 48	12 3	3 39	..		7 4
7½	Marishes Road	..	..	11 17	..	4 12	6 12	..		9¼	Goathland	7 33	8 16	9 58	1213	3 49	..		7 14
11	Pickering	5B46	..	11 27	2 20	4 20	6 19	..		18½	Levisham	7 50	..	10 15	1230	4 6	..		7 31
17	Levisham	5 57	..	11 38	2 31	4 31	6 30	..		24¼	Pickering	8 5	..	10 29	1242	4 20	725		7 45
25¼	Goathland	6 14	8 25	11 55	2 48	4 48	6 47	..		27¼	Marishes Road	8 11	..	1248	..	..	..		7 51
29	Grosmont	6 26	8 32	12 2	3 56	4 55	6 54	..		35½	Malton .... arr	8 22	..	10 44	1259	4 35	745		8 2
32½	Sleights	..	8 41	12 11	3 55	4 7	3	..		56½	109 York .... arr	9L 9	..	11N35	1 54	5 25	825	9	6
33½	Ruswarp	Aa	8 46	12 16	3 10	5	9 7	8	..		81¾	116 Leeds (City) .. ″	9 55	..	12 30	2 24	6 37	949	10	0
35½	Whitby .... arr	6 40	8 50	12 21	3 14	5	137	12	..		136½	103 Newcastle .. ″	1215	..	2 31	5	6 9	X 5	..	11 11

A Dep. 9 20 a.m. on Saturdays.   Aa Calls when required to set down from York.
C Through train between York and Whitby on Mondays and Saturdays.   F Dep. 1 15 p.m. on Saturdays.
J Dep. 10 25 a.m. on Mondays and Saturdays.   K Dep. 3 10 p.m. on Mondays and Saturdays.   L Arr. 8 55 a.m. on Mondays and Saturdays.   N Arr. 11 17 a.m. on Mondays and Saturdays.   P Dep. 11 30 a.m. commencing 20th September.   p.m.   R Dep. 2 0 p.m. on Saturdays until 27th September inclusive.   S Saturdays only.
U Arr. 2 45 p.m. on 4th October.   V Dep. 2 38 p.m. on Saturdays 28th June to 30th August inclusive.   X Arr. 8 45 p.m. on Fridays.

For OTHER TRAINS between York and Pickering, see Table 113—Grosmont and Whitby, Table 131.

Table 111 — MALTON and DRIFFIELD

Miles		Week Days only							Miles		Week Days only						
		a.m		a.m	p.m						a.m		p.m	p.m			
—	Malton .... dep	7 0	..	11 10	5 55	..	..		—	Driffield .... dep	8 56	..	12 25	7 30	..	..	
3½	Settrington	7 8		11 18	6 3	..	..		3½	Garton	9 3		12 32	7 37	..	..	
4½	North Grimston	7 11		11 21	6 6	..	..		6½	Wetwang	9 9		12 38	7 43	..	..	
6½	Wharram	7 16	Saturdays	11 26	6 11	..	..		8½	Sledmere and Fimber..	9 14	Saturdays	12 43	7 48	..	..	
9	Burdale	7 21		11 31	6 16	..	..		11	Burdale	9 20		12 49	7 54	..	..	
11½	Sledmere and Fimber..	7 26		11 36	6 21	..	..		13½	Wharram	9 25		12 54	7 59	..	..	
13½	Wetwang	7 30		11 40	6 25	..	..		15½	North Grimston	9 29		12 58	8 3	..	..	
16½	Garton	7 36		11 46	6 31	..	..		16½	Settrington	9 32		1 1	8 6	..	..	
20	Driffield .... arr	7 42		11 55	6 37	..	..		20	Malton .... arr	9 39		1 8	8 15	..	..	

Table 112 — SCARBOROUGH and PICKERING (One class only)

Miles		Week Days only						Miles		Week Days only					
		a.m	p.m		p.m					a.m		a.m	p.m		
—	Scarborough (Cen.). dep	8 40	2 50	..	6 30	..		—	Pickering .... dep	7 0	..	9 43	5 10	..	..
3	Seamer	8 47	2 57	..	6 37	..		3	Thornton Dale	7 7	..	9 51	5 17	..	..
6½	Forge Valley	8 55	3 5	..	6 46	..		5½	Ebberston	7 13	..	9 57	5 23	..	..
8	Wykeham	9 0	3 9	..	6 50	..		8½	Snainton	7 19	..	10 3	5 31	..	..
9½	Sawdon	9 5	3 14	..	6 56	..		10	Sawdon	7 24	..	10 8	5 36	..	..
11½	Snainton	9 10	3 19	..	7 1	..		11½	Wykeham	7 30	..	10 13	5 41	..	..
14	Ebberston	9 16	3 25	..	7 7	..		13½	Forge Valley	7 35	..	10 17	5 45	..	..
16½	Thornton Dale	9 22	3 31	..	7 13	..		16½	Seamer	7 44	..	10 26	5 53	..	..
19½	Pickering .... arr	9 30	3 38	..	7 20	..		19½	Scarborough (Cen.). arr	7 50	..	10 32	5 59	..	..

For OTHER TRAINS between Scarborough & Seamer, see Tables 105 and 109

The timetable issued by the LNER covering the period from 16 June to 5 October 1947. Table 110 records the services over the line from Malton to Whitby – including the line from Pickering to Grosmont that survives as today's preserved North Yorkshire Moors Railway – whilst Table 112 demonstrates the three return workings per day over the Forge Valley line from Scarborough to Pickering. Tables 107 and 108 (shown on the next page) cover the services over the coastal route from Loftus to Scarborough and that linking the two stations in Whitby. *Author's collection*

Table 107 SCARBOROUGH, WHITBY, SALTBURN, and MIDDLESBROUGH

Miles		Week Days a.m	p.m.	a.m S	a.m S	a.m.		a.m S	p.m S	a.m S	a.m	p.m		Sundays a.m	p.m	p.m
	109 London (K.C.) dep	..	10N40	..	..	4 25	..	..	..	9 30	10 0	1 0	..	10†30	..	..
	109 York .... "	..	4a30	..	9A35	10 15	..	10B55	1H 2	1p20	3p 5	6 25	..	9 10	5 0	..
—	**Scarborough (Cen.)** dep	..	8 12	..	11 0	11 38	..	1p 0	2 25	4 0	4 33	8 5	..	10 50	6 55	..
2¾	Scalby	..	8 27	..	..	11 52	..	..	..	..	4 47	8 19	..	11 4	7 9	..
5	Cloughton	..	8 32	..	..	11 57	..	..	2 45	4 20	4 52	8 24	..	11 9	7 14	..
7	Hayburn Wyke	..	8 37	..	..	12 2	..	..	2 50	..	4J57	8 29	..	11 14	7 19	..
8	Stainton Dale	..	8 41	..	..	12 10	..	..	2 54	..	5 1	8 33	..	11 18	7 23	..
10¼	Ravenscar	..	8 51	..	..	12 19	..	1 38	3 3	..	5 12	8 42	..	11 27	7 32	..
13½	Fyling Hall	..	8 59	..	..	12 27	..	..	..	..	5 20	..	..	..	..	..
15¼	Robin Hood's Bay	..	9 4	..	1147	12 32	..	1 57	3 16	4 50	5 25	8 55	..	11 40	7 46	..
18½	Hawsker	..	9 13	..	..	12 41	..	..	..	..	5 34	9 4	..	11 49	7 55	..
21¾	**Whitby West Cliff** arr	..	9 20	..	12 2	12 48	..	2 12	3 31	5 5	5 41	9 11	..	11 56	8 2	..
23½	**Whitby** arr	..	9 42	..	..	..	..	..	..	..	..	9 22	..	..	8 13	..
	Whitby dep	6 55	..	9 20	..	..	..	..	..	..	..	..	..	..	..	..
—	**Whitby West Cliff** dep	7 3	..	9 30	12 7	12 51	..	2 20	3 35	5 10	5 44	..	..	12 2	..	8 15
24	Sandsend	7 9	..	9 36	1213	12 57	..	2 26	3 41	5 16	5 50	..	..	12 8	..	8 21
26¾	Kettleness....[wick Bay	7 17	..	9 44	1221	1 5	..	2 39	3 49	5 24	5 59	..	..	12 15	..	8 28
30	Hinderwell, for Runs-	7 25	..	9 52	1229	1 13	..	2 47	3 57	5 32	6 7	..	..	12 23	..	8 36
31¾	Staithes	7 31	..	9 57	1234	1 18	..	2 52	4 2	5 41	6 12	..	..	12 28	..	8 41
36¾	Loftus	7 49	..	1015	1252	1 33	..	..	4 17	5 56	6 27	..	..	12 43	..	8 56
37½	Skinningrove	7 53	..	1019	..	1 37	..	..	..	..	6 31	..	..	12 47	..	9 0
41¼	Brotton	8 4	..	1030	..	1 48	..	..	..	..	6 40	..	..	12 56	..	9 9
45½	139 Saltburn ..... arr	..	..	1052	..	..	..	..	..	..	7 7	..	..	..	..	..
58	**Middlesbrough** .... arr	8 46	..	1112	1 33	2 31	..	3 48	5R21	6 43	7 22	..	..	1 37	..	9 50

Miles		Week Days a.m.	a.m S	a.m S	a.m	a.m	a.m S	p.m S	p.m S	p.m	p.m	p.m S		Sundays a.m	p.m	p m
	Middlesbrough ..... dep	6 15	8 0	8R45	9 38	..	1040	12 5	1 7	..	4 20	8 32	..	1015	..	5 50
	139 Saltburn ...... dep	..	..	..	9 50	..	..	..	..	..	..	..	..	..	..	..
16¾	Brotton	7 0	..	..	1024	..	..	..	1 53	..	5 7	9 21	..	11 1	..	6 36
20½	Skinningrove	7 9	..	..	1033	..	..	..	2 2	..	5 17	9 30	..	1110	..	6 45
21¼	Loftus	7 16	..	9 33	1041	..	..	1250	2 10	..	5 24	9 38	..	1115	..	6 50
26¼	Staithes......[wick Bay	7 32	..	..	1055	..	..	1 4	2 24	..	5F42	9 52	..	1129	..	7 4
28	Hinderwell, for Runs-	7 38	..	9 53	11 1	..	..	1 14	2 30	..	5 48	9 58	..	1135	..	7 10
31¼	Kettleness	7 46	..	10 1	11 9	..	..	..	2 38	..	6 0	10 6	..	1143	..	7 18
34	Sandsend	7 53	..	10 8	1116	..	..	..	2 45	..	6 8	1013	..	1150	..	7 25
36¼	**Whitby West Cliff** arr	7 59	9 17	1014	1122	..	12 5	1 32	2 51	..	6 14	1019	..	1156	..	7 31
38	**Whitby** arr	..	..	..	1130	..	..	..	3 0	..	..	1027	..	..	..	..
	Whitby dep	..	..	..	..	1115	..	..	..	4 20	..	..	..	..	5 0	..
—	**Whitby West Cliff** dep	8 12	9 21	1025	..	1129	1210	1 37	..	4 31	6 19	..	..	12 0	5 11	..
39½	Hawsker	8 21	..	..	..	1138	..	..	..	4 41	6 28	..	..	12 9	5 20	..
42¾	Robin Hood's Bay	8 30	9 39	1043	..	1146	1233	1 55	..	4 49	6 37	..	..	1219	5 30	..
44½	Fyling Hall	8 35	..	..	..	1151	..	..	..	4 54	..	..	..	..	..	..
47¾	Ravenscar	8 53	..	11 1	..	12 4	1250	2 12	..	5 13	6 54	..	..	1234	5 45	..
50	Stainton Dale	8 58	..	11 6	..	12 9	..	..	..	5 18	6 59	..	..	1239	5 50	..
51	Hayburn Wyke	9 2	..	11 9	..	1212	..	2 20	..	5 21	7 3	..	..	1243	5 54	..
53	Cloughton	9 7	..	1117	..	1217	1 1	2 25	..	5 25	7 8	..	..	1248	6 0	..
55¼	Scalby	9 12	..	..	..	1222	..	..	..	5 30	7 13	..	..	1253	6 5	..
58	**Scarborough (Cen.)** arr	9 25	1016	1129	..	1235	1 13	2 38	..	5 43	7 26	..	..	1 2	6 14	..
100	109 York .... arr	11 35	1135	1 54	..	1 54	3B10	5 25	..	8 25	9 6	..	..	..	8 30	..
288	109 London (K.C.) "	3 25	3 25	..	..	6C50	..	9 30	..	..	2a49	..	..	..	2a49	..

NOTES

- **A** Dep. 8 58 a.m. on 4th October
- *a* a.m.
- **B** Except 4th October
- **C** Arr. 5 47 p.m. on Saturdays
- **F** Arr. 5 37 p.m.
- **H** Dep. 12 20 p.m. on 20th and 27th September and 4th October
- **J** Stops to set down only
- **N** Dep. 10 45 p.m on Sundays
- *p* p.m.
- **R** Via Redcar (Table 135)
- † Saturday nights

For **LOCAL TRAINS** and **intermediate Stations** between Brotton and Middlesbrough, see Table 134.

Table 108 WHITBY and WHITBY WEST CLIFF

Miles		Week Days a.m	a.m S	a.m	p.m			Suns. p.m	
—	**Whitby** .... dep	6 55	9 20	1115	4 20	..	..	5 0	..
1¼	**Whitby West Cliff.** arr	7 1	9 26	1121	4 26	..	..	5 6	..

Miles		Week Days a.m	a.m	p.m S	p.m	p.m S	Suns. p.m	
—	**Whitby West Cliff.** dep	9 36	1124	2 54	9 16	1021	8 7	..
1¼	**Whitby** .... arr	9 42	1130	3 0	9 22	1027	8 13	..

S Saturdays only

nature of the company and poor construction of the line (by John Dickson), the project had to be rescued by the NER (which took out a lease on the line from 1 July 1875) and it was not opened until 3 December 1883. The final link in the local network came with the opening of the line from Whitby to Scarborough on 16 July 1885.

Apart from the loss of the Beckholes passenger service, the entire network passed via the NER and LNER to British Railways (North Eastern Region) with the exception of local services over the Gilling to Malton section which had ceased on 1 January 1931 (although the route remained open for excursion traffic and other specials until 1964). However, it was not long before the process of further contraction commenced. The first casualty was the passenger service on the Forge Valley line; this had been operated by Sentinel railcars before World War 2 but these had been replaced by locomotive-hauled sets and services ceased on 3 January 1950. The line east of Thornton Dale was closed completely at the same time.

This was followed on 2 February 1953 by the withdrawal of passenger services on the line from Pilmoor via Gilling to Pickering; the section east of Kirbymoorside was also to close completely at the same time. Until 1964 the rump of the line was used regularly by excursions and other specials. The line west of Battersby to Picton lost its passenger services on 14 June 1954. The section between Picton and Stokesley was closed completely on 1 December 1958; the section from Stokesley to Battersby closed completely on 2 August 1965.

The line north from Whitby West Cliff to Loftus closed completely on 3 May 1958; thereafter, services from Scarborough to Middlesbrough (which had been converted to DMU operation at the same time) were diverted to reverse at West Cliff and again at Town stations until West Cliff itself closed on 12 June 1961 when the reversal was made at Prospect Hill Junction.

The Beeching report – *The Reshaping of British Railways* – was published in March 1963; it proposed the closure of the three routes to Whitby; there was the inevitable outcry and, following the review of the objections, consent was given to the closure of the lines from Grosmont to Malton and from Whitby to Scarborough; both lines – with the exception of the section from Pickering to Rillington (which was retained for freight traffic until 1 July 1966) – closed completely on 8 March 1965.

Between the publication of the Beeching report and the closures of March 1965, many of the routes that had survived for freight traffic only also succumbed. Stone traffic ceased to be shipped from Thornton Dale on 21 January 1963 although it was not until 10 August 1964 that the line was officially closed. The same day witnessed the withdrawal of freight from the lines from Kirbymoorside to Gilling and from Husthwaite Gate to Amotherby (the section from Husthwaite Gate west to Pilmoor had already closed – on 10 September 1962). The short section to Amotherby from Malton survived until 19 October 1964.

The Esk Valley line, however, was to survive; although the route has been considerably rationalised, it still provides an essential link between the town and Middlesbrough.

In 1967, faced by the imminent lifting of the track on the routes from Grosmont to Rillington Junction and from Whitby to Scarborough, a group to try and preserve one route was established. Examining both led to a decision to concentrate on the route to Pickering. On 22 April 1973 the North Yorkshire Moors Railway commenced operation between Pickering and Grosmont; from 3 April 2007, following agreement with Network Rail and route training, these services were extended into Whitby (although there had been earlier one-off services operated prior to that date). More than 170 years after the opening the Whitby & Pickering Railway a regular through service between the towns was restored.

The junction off the line from Pickering towards Malton for the Forge Valley and Gilling branches was at Mill Lane. This was situated about half-a-mile south of the station. Pictured at the junction between the Forge Valley line, seen curving away to the east in the background, and the main line southwards is 'Shire' class 4-4-0 No 62730 *Berkshire*. The locomotive was allocated to York (North) between October 1950 and August 1958, before a final transfer took the locomotive to Selby, from where it was withdrawn four months later. When the Forge Valley and Gilling lines were opened, both originally had double-track junctions with the main line; this was normal NER practice when the lines were built but, in 1924, both branches were modified to operate as single track with the second line being retained solely for use as a siding. The junction was originally opened with the branch to Gilling on 1 April 1875. The NER signalbox was demolished after the closure of the Pickering to Rillington Junction section on 1 July 1966. *Neville Stead Collection/Transport Treasury*

The York & North Midland Railway opened the first engine shed at Pickering, on the section of line between the station and junction, on 7 July 1845. The single-road shed was extended by the NER in 1876. The shed – seen here from the south – closed on 6 April 1959.

The building is still extant, albeit now incorporated into a much larger structure, as part of the premises occupied by the joinery company S. Taylor & Son Ltd.
Neville Stead Collection/Transport Treasury

Between Pickering station and the box controlling Mill Lane Junction, there were two other signalboxes in a distance of only just over 700 yards. The northernmost of these two boxes was Bridge Street, seen here in a derelict condition after the line's closure, which was sited only 140 yards south of the box that controlled Pickering station. Bridge Street and Hungate, a further 160 yards to the south, were both decommissioned with the final closure of route on 1 July 1966.
Norris Forrest/Transport Treasury

Although the original station opened in Pickering with the completion of the Whitby & Pickering Railway in 1835, the station that exists today – which is now Grade II listed – was designed by the York & North Midland Railway's architect G. T. Andrews and completed in 1846. When viewed from the south on 27 May 1950, the station still retained its overall roof; this was, however, removed by British Railways during 1952. Following the closure of the Grosmont to Pickering and thence to Rillington Junction section on 8 March 1965 on 1 July 1966 (when freight traffic to Pickering New Bridge ceased) respectively, Pickering was later to become the southern terminus of the preserved North Yorkshire Moors Railway. The preserved railway undertook the restoration of the overall roof, with work being completed in 2011.
Tony Wickens/Online Transport Archive

On 13 April 1964 the preserved Class K4 3442 (ex-BR No 61994) *The Great Marquess*, restored to LNER livery, was used by the BBC on a filming special between Leeds and Whitby (and return) via Pickering. Here, the train is seen approaching Pickering station from the south. The three-cylinder 'K4' class was designed by Nigel Gresley for use on the ex-North British West Highland line. Six locomotives, BR Nos 61993-98, were constructed at Darlington Works between January 1937 and January 1939. Following withdrawal in December 1961, No 61994 (which had carried the name *MacCailein Mór* briefly when new in July 1938 before being renamed later the same month) was preserved by Viscount Garnock. Restored at Cowlairs Works to LNER livery, the locomotive hauled a freight to Neville Hill, in Leeds, during April 1963, where it was to be based for the next nine years. Used on a number of specials between 1963 and 1967, when it was withdrawn for a boiler repair, No 3442 was to make a return trip to the Malton to Whitby line on 6 March 1965 when it and 'K1' class 62005 (later itself to be preserved) operated the joint Stephenson Locomotive Society/Manchester Locomotive Society 'Whitby Moors' railtour from Manchester Victoria; this special was to be one of the last passenger services to traverse the route south from Grosmont until the line was reopened by the North Yorkshire Moors Railway. *Gavin Morrison*

Whilst the incoming Labour government of October 1964 did not reverse Ernest Marples's decision, taken the previous month, to confirm the closure of the line from Grosmont to Malton, the new Minister of Transport, Tom Fraser, did stipulate that the track must be left in situ for a period. This is the view looking towards Pickering station after closure and shows the weed-infested track. On the platforms of the disused station can be seen the short platform canopies erected by BR following the removal of the overall roof in 1952; these were themselves removed as part of the project to restore the station. In June 1967 BR intimated in a letter to Whitby RDC that, as it was unlikely that financial support for the line's reopening would be forthcoming from the local authorities, it proposed to start the lifting of the line that summer. However, the first stirrings of a preservation scheme had already arisen and this resulted in a delay to the proposed lifting. BR quoted the sum of £120,000 (equivalent to £1.5 million at today's prices) for the route and infrastructure from Grosmont to Pickering. In May 1969 a 10% deposit for the purchase price of a reduced scheme – the track from Grosmont to Ellerbeck and the trackbed thence to Pickering – was handed over; however, additional financial support was offered and the entire line was secured. The section south from Pickering to Rillington Junction was lifted in 1969.
Norris Forrest/Transport Treasury

York (North) (50A)-allocated 'Shire' class 4-4-0 No 62731 *Selkirkshire* heads south from Levisham with a service towards Pickering and Rillington Junction. The 'D49' was completed as LNER No 2756 at Darlington Works in March 1929. It was renumbered 2731 as part of the LNER's renumbering scheme in June 1946. It was first allocated to York (North) in October 1950 and was to spend the next seven years, except for a few months during 1955 when it was based at Starbeck, at Malton, Scarborough or York (North). A final transfer, in July 1957, took the locomotive to Selby, from where it as withdrawn in April 1959.
Neville Stead Collection/Transport Treasury

As a southbound DMU heads into Levisham, the token for the single-line section on to Pickering is ready. The first DMUs to operate over the Whitby to Malton line appeared in 1958 with the majority of services over the route being DMU operated from May 1959; locomotive-hauled services were restricted to morning and evening services that conveyed parcels and mail. Generally there were five return workings per day at the time with a sixth added during the summer months. There were also two shuttles from Whitby to Goathland. In February 1964 BR issued closure notices for the three routes to Whitby; of the trio, the Malton line was the biggest loss maker, losing more than £49,000 per annum (for each £1 of revenue it incurred £2.45 of operating costs). On 8 and 9 July 1964 the Transport Users Consultative Committee held a hearing into the proposed closures following the inevitable objections. On 11 September 1964 the then Minister of Transport, Ernest Marples, announced a reprieve for the Esk Valley line but, despite the election of a new Labour government in the election of 16 October 1964, there was to be no change of heart as far as the Malton line was concerned.

Yorkshire Post/Transport Treasury

On 6 July 1952 the track gang unloads ballast near Goathland; the train is hauled by Class J25 0-6-0 No 65690. This class was designed by William Worsdell with a total of 120 being constructed between 1898 and 1902; two-thirds were built at Gateshead Works with the remainder at Darlington. No 65690 was one of those completed at Gateshead – in January 1900 – as NER No 2091; it was renumbered 5690 in October 1946. During World War 2 40 of the type were loaned to the GWR to replace 'Dean Goods' 0-6-0s that had been requisitioned by the War Department; this included No 2091, which was transferred to the GWR in October 1939 and was not to return to the LNER until January 1946. Transferred from Hull (Dairycoates) to Whitby in January 1951, it was withdrawn from the latter shed in November 1954.
Tony Wickens/Online Transport Archive

Viewed from the south with a three-car DMU awaiting departure in the down platform, the extensive facilities provided at Goathland station are clearly evident. The sidings on the east side of the station originally served a quarry that was linked to the railway by a short narrow gauge railway; the quarry ceased operations in 1951 although operation of the narrow gauge railway had ceased during the previous decade. Freight facilities were withdrawn from Goathland on 27 April 1964; passenger services were withdrawn on Monday 8 March 1965. Although the new Labour Minster of Transport, Tom Fraser, after the October 1964 election refused to reverse the closure, the ministerial instruction for this – and other already approved closures – was that the track and infrastructure be retained. This was followed and, on 29 and 30 November 1965, BR operated emergency services for schoolchildren from Goathland to Whitby and return as a result of a heavy snowfall that prevented the running of the usual schoolbuses. The retention of the track was a factor in the successful reopening of the North Yorkshire Moors Railway following the establishment of the preservation society in 1967.

Neville Stead Collection/Transport Treasury

In the mid-1950s a Class J25 0-6-0 ascends the gradient on the approaches to Goathland with a southbound freight. Having departed from Grosmont, the train has been ascending for about 3½ miles, the bulk at 1 in 49; beyond the station, the locomotive crew is faced by a further ascent for a further two miles to reach the summit of the line at Ellerbeck, some 632ft above sea level, from there the route descends all the way through to Pickering and Rillington Junction.

Neville Stead Collection/Transport Treasury

In August 1949 Class J24 No 65628 – one of only a handful of the class to receive its BR number – is pictured heading a down freight through Grosmont towards the junction with the line towards Pickering and onwards to Whitby. Completed as NER No 1934 in December 1897 at Gateshead, the locomotive retained its original number at Grouping before being renumbered 5628 in 1946. It was renumbered whilst at Darlington Works for modification in February 1949 and was then reallocated to Whitby shed, from where it was withdrawn in November 1950.
Neil Davenport/Online Transport Archive

In 1958 Fairburn 2-6-4T No 42083 arrives in Sleights with an up service from Whitby. The original station was provided in 1835 by the Whitby & Pickering Railway but the station that exists today is the result of the modernisation of the route following its acquisition by the York & North Midland Railway on 30 June 1845. The new station was designed by G. T. Andrews and opened in 1846. The layout at the station was rationalised in 1984 when the down platform was decommissioned and the signalbox closed and demolished. The main station building, which is now Grade II listed, is now in use as a private residence. No 42083 was constructed at Brighton Works in February 1951; allocated to Whitby between October 1955 and April 1959, it was transferred to York (North). Its final shed was Normanton, from where it was withdrawn in October 1967. Two of the class – Nos 42073 and 42085 – survive in preservation and are based on the Lakeside & Haverthwaite Railway. *Neville Stead Collection/Transport Treasury*

With Larpool viaduct in the background, Class B1 No 61154 is pictured crossing the River Esk at Ruswarp with a westbound service toward Grosmont. The station at Ruswarp is beyond the signalbox on the north bank of the river and traffic on the road bridge is waiting for the train to clear the level crossing before heading into Ruswarp itself on the B1416. No 61154 was new from Vulcan Foundry as LNER No 1154 in May 1947 and, from June 1947 through to withdrawal in September 1962, was allocated to Sheffield (Darnall) shed. The locomotive's presence on the Esk Valley line was, thus, well away from its usual haunts and was probably the result of a running-in turn following work undertaken at Darlington Works, where the locomotive received attention on four occasions between 1952 and 1957.
Neville Stead Collection/Transport Treasury

The imposing Larpool viaduct seen from the carriage window in August 1949. The 13-arch single-track viaduct, which is 305 yards in length, was constructed in brick. Work started on its construction in October 1882 with work taking two years. The resident engineer was Charles Rowlandson, with construction being handled by John Waddell & Sons. The construction of the viaduct was influenced by the fact that the River Esk is tidal at this point with three of the piers being skewed to avoid any deflection of the tidal flow. As can be seen in this view, a number of the piers had tripe or double foundations, which were connected above the water level by semi-circular arches. Traffic over the viaduct ceased in 1965 and, seven years later, the viaduct was given protection when it became Grade II listed. The viaduct, which underwent significant restoration a decade or so ago, is now part of the footpath and cycleway that makes use of much of the redundant trackbed between Whitby and Scarborough.
Neil Davenport/Online Transport Archive

The signabox at Whitby Town, seen here in 1967, was unusual in being of three storeys; this was constructed in 1876 when block signalling was introduced to the line in place of the time interval system. The additional height was required so that the signalman could see over the adjacent goods shed. The box closed in 1984 when the layout was rationalised and was subsequently demolished.
Neville Stead Collection/Online Transport Archive

In August 1949 Class G5 0-4-4T No E7335 stands outside the ex-NER shed at Whitby. The class was designed by William Worsdell for light passenger work; a total of 110 were constructed between May 1894 and December 1901 at Darlington Works with this example emerging in June 1901 as NER No 1319. Renumbered 7335 in March 1946 as part of the LNER's renumbering scheme, it was finally to gain its BR identity in June 1950. Allocated to Whitby, No 67335 was withdrawn in August 1953. The original shed at Whitby had its origins with one constructed for the York & North Midland Railway that opened on 6 June 1847. This single-road shed was rebuilt as a two-road shed in 1868 and was further modified in 1903. The facilities provided included a turntable – enlarged to 60ft in 1936 – a water column and coal stage. The shed, which is now Grade II listed, was closed by BR on 6 April 1959 – a consequence of the introduction of DMUs to local passenger services – although the building remains and is now in commercial use.

Neil Davenport/Online Transport Archive

On 22 August 1949 Class G5 No 7332 – still retaining its LNER identity despite more than 18 months having elapsed since Nationalisation (it would finally become BR No 67332 in October 1949) – is seen light engine in Whitby Town station. The station at Whitby was designed for the York & North Midland Railway by G. T. Andrews; it replaced an older station provided for the Whitby & Pickering and opened on 4 June 1847. When recorded here, the station retained its overall roof; this was, however, removed by BR during 1953 and replaced by platform awnings. The stone-built station, with its five-arched Romanesque portico, remains and is now Grade II listed. No 7332 was completed as NER No 468 at Darlington Works in June 1901; renumbered 7332 in October 1946 as part of the LNER's renumbering scheme, when recorded here it was a relatively recent arrival in the district, having been transferred from Starbeck to Malton in May 1949. It was to remain allocated to Malton until withdrawal in April 1956. The last of the 'G5' 0-4-4Ts were withdrawn in late 1958. Although none were preserved at the time, work is in hand at the time of writing on the construction of a new example.

Neil Davenport/Online Transport Archive

A busy view of Whitby Town station in 1958 records one of the then newly-introduced DMUs in platform 1 with Class L1 No 67754 standing at the head of a train in platform 2 whilst BR Standard Class 3MT 2-6-0 No 77012 occupies the station siding. Whitby at the time possessed four platforms; the two illustrated in this view plus two shorter platforms to the south; the latter were later removed and the site redeveloped as a supermarket. Although the layout at Whitby was considerably rationalised, work undertaken about a decade ago resulted in enhanced facilities as part of a project to facilitate greater use of the station by services operated from Grosmont to Whitby by the North Yorkshire Moors Railway. No 77012, one of 20 of the type constructed by Swindon Works during 1954, was allocated to Whitby shed between December 1955 and December 1958; it was to end its days in April 1966 allocated to York (North). No 67754 was one of the North British-built batch of 'L1s' and was completed in December 1958. When pictured here it was allocated to Middlesbrough and was to remain on Tees-side until December 1961 when a final reallocation saw it move to Low Moor, from where it was withdrawn in November 1962.
Neville Stead Collection/Transport Treasury

A two-car DMU with E50252 leading is pictured departing from Whitby with a service to Scarborough. In 1957, following their construction at Metro-Cammell, 10 two-car units (later designated as Class 101) – Nos E50250-59 with Nos E50260-69 – were allocated to Darlington shed and made their appearance on services to and from Whitby. The closure of the Loftus to Whitby West Cliff section in 1958 resulted in the recasting of the timetable and led to the introduction of DMUs to the route from Middlesbrough to Scarborough via Whitby. The arrival of the DMUs had an impact on the economics of many of the lines to which they were allocated and certainly made operation of the route to Scarborough, with its reversal at Prospect Hill Junction, much more straightforward. Unfortunately, it was perhaps a case of too little, too late as publication of the Beeching Report in March 1963 listed the route to Scarborough as one of those to be closed. Indeed, despite the introduction of DMUs to the other routes, all three of the lines serving Whitby were slated for closure; in the event, however, the Esk Valley line was reprieved.
Yorkshire Post/Transport Treasury

In 1957, Class L1 2-6-4T No 67765 descends under Larpool Viaduct with a service towards Whitby Town. Completed at North British in February 1949 – the last of 36 of the class to be built there – No 67765 was allocated to Whitby for two months – from mid-January to mid-March – in 1957 sandwiched between two periods when allocated to Middlesbrough. Spending most of its operational life in and around Tees-side, the locomotive was transferred to Ardsley in December 1961 from where it was withdrawn in November the following year. The connection from Prospect Hill Junction to Bog Hall Junction was closed with the withdrawal of passenger services between Whitby and Scarborough on 6 March 1965. More than 50 years after closure, the formation, albeit heavily overgrown, remains intact. South from Prospect Hill Junction and over the viaduct, the railway has been converted into a public footpath. *Neville Stead Collection/Transport Treasury*

As a member of the footplate crew prepares to hand over the single-line token, Class L1 No 67754 approaches Whitby West Cliff station from the south on 3 May 1958. This was the last day of services through West Cliff towards Loftus. Thereafter, West Cliff station remained open to serve trains on the route from Scarborough until 10 June 1961, when the Scarborough services reached Prospect Hill Junction to reverse down to Whitby Town station and passenger facilities were withdrawn from West Cliff.

The station buildings at West Cliff survive, having been converted into private housing. A total of 100 of Edward Thompson's class of 2-6-4T were built in 1945 (when the prototype was completed) and between 1948 and 1950. No 67754 was built by North British in December 1948 and survived until withdrawal in November 1962. All of the class had been withdrawn by the end of that year.
Tony Wickens/Online Transport Archive

BR Standard 2-6-4T No 80118 is pictured standing in the southbound platforms at Whitby West Cliff station. Although the photograph is undated, it probably dates to the period between June 1955, when No 80118 was allocated new to Whitby shed (having been completed at Brighton Works earlier in the month), and June 1958, when the locomotive was transferred to Neville Hill. Later in its career, the locomotive was transferred to Scottish Region, being withdrawn from Polmadie shed in May 1964. Passenger services north from West Cliff to Loftus were withdrawn on 5 May 1958, towards the end of No 80118's sojourn on the Yorkshire coast. *Neville Stead Collection/Transport Treasury*

In August 1949 Class A8 4-6-2T No 69858 heads northwards over the viaduct at Sandsend as it approaches the small one-platform station that served this coastal community. Following the closure of the line north from Whitby West Cliff on 5 May 1958, the track between Whitby and Loftus was lifted during 1959 and the viaduct demolished the following year. The viaduct at Sandsend was one of five – the others being at Upgang, Newholm Bank, East Row and Staithes – that were constructed in tubular steel for the Whitby, Redcar & Middlesbrough Union Railway. All were demolished following the line's closure. No 69858 was completed as NER No 2151 at Darlington Works in December 1913; retained its original number at Grouping in 1923, it was renumbered 9858 in October 1946 as part of the LNER's renumbering scheme and, when recorded here, was allocated to Whitby shed. Transferred to Leeds (Neville Hill) in June 1954, it then spent some time at Hull (Botanic Gardens) and Middlesbrough before being withdrawn from Sunderland in May 1959.

Neil Davenport/Online Transport Archive

With the viaduct visible to the south, this view of Sandsend station was taken in 1958 and thus captures the view contemporaneously with the closure of the route north from Whitby West Cliff. The station opened with the line on 3 December 1883. The station had one siding – to the north of the station – which provided access to the coal drops. This was the only freight dealt with at Sandsend although more extensive facilities, along with a goods shed, were provided at East Row, to the south of the viaduct. In later years – between 1955 and 1958 – three camping coaches were based on the siding; following the line's closure, these were removed and transferred to locations on the line between Whitby and Scarborough. Following closure, the brick-built station was converted into a private house. It and the coal drops – now converted into garages – survive.
Neville Stead Collection/Transport Treasury

In August 1949 Class J24 0-6-0 No 5621 – still bearing its final LNER number more than 18 months after Nationalisation – is pictured with a freight in the down platform at Robin Hood's Bay. The 'J24' type was designed by William Worsdell and first entered service in 1894; a total of 70 were constructed between then and 1898. Although the first of the class had been withdrawn in 1933, a total of 34 survived to pass into BR ownership in January 1948. All, however, had been withdrawn by the end of 1951; No 5621 – which never received its allocated BR number – was taken out of service in September 1950.
Neil Davenport/Online Transport Archive

A three-car Derby-built DMU heads north from Robin Hood's Bay with a service towards Middlesbrough. Historically this service would have headed from Whitby West Cliff via Loftus but, following the closure of the coastal route, the journey now required three reversals at Whitby West Cliff, Whitby Town and Battersby. In the background can be seen some of the camping coaches provided at the station. Following World War 2, camping coaches were restored to a number of stations in 1952; three were allocated to Robin Hood's Bay between 1955 and 1958 and this was increased to five between 1959 and 1964 when a number of those allocated to the section north of West Cliff were transferred south. The camping coaches were all withdrawn at the end of the 1964 season. The goods yard at Robin Hood's Bay was the most extensive on the line between Whitby and Scarborough; facilities included five sidings, a goods shed and a coal yard. Although most stations along the section lost their freight facilities in May 1964, those at Robin Hood's Bay were to survive until 10 August 1964. *Neville Stead Collection/Transport Treasury*

On 7 August 1957 Class A8 69867 is pictured with the 11.40am service from Scarborough to Middlesbrough, having just passed through the tunnel at Ravenscar. The tunnel was single track and extended for 279 yards; it was located slightly to the west of Ravenscar station with quite a sharp curve that required a check rail. No 69867, originally NER No 2160, was constructed at Darlington Works as a 4-4-4T in March 1914; it was rebuilt as a 4-6-2T in July 1936. As part of the LNER renumbering scheme it became No 9867 in February 1946. Allocated to Scarborough, Selby and Hull (Botanic Gardens) at various stages during the 1950s, it was taken out of service from Scarborough in May 1959 but not officially withdrawn until December the same year. *Mike Mitchell/Transport Treasury*

Viewed in Stainton Dale station looking towards the north are Nos 42085 and 61131 on a southbound journey towards Scarborough. The station, which was known as Staintondale until 3 May 1937, opened with the line on 16 July 1885. In later years, the station was one of those on the line – the others being Scalby, Cloughton, Ravenscar and Robin Hood's Bay – that accommodated a camping coach, with one being located in the goods bay. Freight facilities at Stainton Dale were withdrawn on 4 May 1964 with the station closing completely with the withdrawal of passenger services on 8 March 1965. Following closure, the main station buildings were converted into a private house. Designed by

Charles Fairburn, a total of 277 of this 2-6-4T were constructed between 1945 and 1951; a number of the later locomotives – including No 42085 – were constructed at Brighton. Between March 1952 and October 1965, when the locomotive was reallocated to Manningham shed, No 42085 was allocated to a number of sheds – including Scarborough and Whitby – on the North Eastern Region. Following withdrawal from Normanton in October 1967 No 42085 was preserved and is now based on the Lakeside & Haverthwaite Railway with sister No 42073.
Neville Stead Collection/Transport Treasury

Located to the south of Stainton Dale station and adjacent to the Hayburn Wyke Hotel, Hayburn Wyke was a fairly basic structure. Originally opened on 17 July 1885, the station platform, which had been sited on the up (ie east) side of the single track, was rebuilt on the west side when the original wooden platform was replaced with a more substantial brick-built structure in 1887. The stationmaster's house was completed five years later. As a wartime economy measure during World War 1 the station was closed on 1 March 1917; it reopened on 2 May 1921. Reduced to the status of a halt on 23 March 1953, the station closed with the withdrawal of passenger services on the Whitby to Scarborough line on 8 March 1965. Seen southbound with a service to Scarborough is 'A8' No 69890. This was amongst the last of the Class H1 4-4-4Ts to be constructed – emerging as NER No 1521 from Darlington Works in December 1921. Rebuilt as a 4-6-2T in October 1935, it became LNER No 9890 under the 1946 renumbering scheme. Allocated to Whitby through much of the BR era, except for a four-month period during 1956 when it was based at York (North), No 69890 was transferred to Malton in June 1957 from where it was withdrawn in January the following year.
Neville Stead Collection/Transport Treasury

The first station north of Scarborough on the line towards Whitby was at Scalby and this view, taken from the south, shows the single platform and main station building. Immediately to the south of the station was Scalby viaduct, which took the line over the sea cut of the River Derwent. Timetabled passenger services to Scalby ceased on 2 March 1953, although occasional trains continued to call at the station to serve the camping coaches that were based at the station – one of which is visible on the extreme left – until 1964. Following the closure of the line, the station at Scalby was demolished and the site redeveloped for housing. The viaduct and the trackbed of the line south from the station remain intact, as does the route north of the village; through the village itself, however, the route has been subsumed into the expanded community. *Neville Stead Collection/Transport Treasury*

On 13 August 1949 two Class B1 4-6-0s are pictured on the approaches to Scarborough station. Departing with an up service is No E1068 whilst waiting to enter the station is No 61181. The former was completed at North British in Glasgow in August 1946 as LNER No 1068; it was temporarily renumbered E1068 in January 1948 and gained its correct BR identity on 14 October 1949. When recorded here, the locomotive was allocated to Hull Dairycoates; it was transferred to Hull Botanic Gardens in February 1954. In June 1959 it moved to Scarborough and then spent brief periods allocated to Darlington, Thornaby and York (North) before being withdrawn from Ardsley in November 1962. No 61181 was built by Vulcan Foundry as LNER No 1181 in July 1947. Allocated from August 1947 until January 1963 to Sheffield Darnall, it was withdrawn in November 1963. Following withdrawal it was transferred to departmental stock and used as a stationary boiler (as No 18) for train heating purposes before being scrapped in December 1965. *Neil Davenport/Online Transport Archive*

No 60918 is pictured on the turntable at Scarborough shed on 13 August 1949. The building behind the locomotive was the second locomotive shed – opened in 1882 – to serve Scarborough and replaced an earlier shed closer to the station. The 1882 shed itself was to be supplanted by a new eight-road shed further to the south. Thereafter the 1882 shed was used for locomotive storage and repair. No 60918 was completed at Darlington Works in August 1941 as LNER No 4889. The 'V2' type represented the first three-cylinder 2-6-2 locomotives to operate on a British railway. Designed by Sir Nigel Gresley, the class was built for express mixed traffic duties and proved to be a great success. In all, 184 locomotives of the type were built between 1936 and 1944. No 4889 was allocated – but never carried – the number 818 under the LNER's first renumbering scheme of 1946 before becoming No 918 in November that same year. Based at York (North) for its entire operational life, No 60918 was withdrawn in October 1962. *Neil Davenport/Online Transport Archive*

On 13 August 1949 Class B16/2 No 61437 is watered at Scarborough shed. Between 1919 and 1924 Darlington Works constructed 70 4-6-0s to the design of Vincent Raven; designated Class S3 by the NER, they became LNER Class B16 at Grouping. Between 1937 and 1940 seven of the class were rebuilt to designs of Nigel Gresley; fitted with Walschaerts valve gear, higher running plates and longer smokeboxes, these locomotives were redesignated as Class B16/2. A further 17 locomotives were modified to the designs of Edward Thompson between 1942 and 1949; these were the 'B16/3' class. All bar one of the locomotives passed to BR in 1948; the one exception was destroyed by enemy action in June 1942. No 61437 had originally been LNER No 2366 when new in January 1923; rebuilt as a 'B16/2' in February 1940, the locomotive spent most of its working life allocated to York (North). The class was regularly used in the summer months on excursion traffic to Scarborough. No 64137 was transferred to Hull (Dairycoates) in December 1962, from where it was withdrawn in June 1964. *Neil Davenport/Online Transport Archive*

On 27 May 1950, Class G5 0-4-4T No 67273 stands in Snainton station with a service from Scarborough via Seamer to Pickering. The principal station on the Forge Valley line, which opened on 1 May 1882, Snainton was the only intermediate station on the route provided with two platforms and a passing loop. By the date of this photograph, closure of the line was already imminent. The last train operated on Saturday 3 June 1950s with the line being officially closed to passenger traffic on the following Monday. The section from Seamer to Thornton Dale was closed completely at the same time although the track was not lifted until a couple of years later. The three-mile section west from Thornton Junction to Pickering remained open to serve a quarry until 10 August 1964. The station building remains extant having been converted into two houses. *Tony Wickens/Online Transport Archive*

Viewed from the east, Ebberston station possessed a single platform with a brick-built station building. The station opened – as Wilton – on 1 May 1882 and was renamed Ebberston on 1 April 1903. The station possessed limited freight facilities; these included sidings, a cattle dock and coal drops. The station closed completely on 5 June 1950 with withdrawal of passenger services on the Forge Valley line and the closure to all traffic of the section east of Thornton Dale. This photograph was taken shortly after the line's closure; the disused track from Thornton Dale to Seamer was lifted in 1953. The station building, now in use as a private house, and other railway structures survive.
Neville Stead Collection/Transport Treasur

The first station heading east from Pickering on the Forge Valley line was Thornton Dale, which served the village of Thornton-le-Dale, which opened with the line on 1 May 1882. This view, taken in 1962 a decade after the line lost its passenger services (on 5 June 1950), records the station from the east with the level crossing beyond the station. By this date, Thornton Dale was the terminus of the line from Pickering; the line east of Thornton Dale was closed completely at the same time as the passenger service was withdrawn with the redundant track being lifted three years later. The section from Pickering to Thornton Dale was retained until 10 August 1964 for stone traffic from a local quarry, although revenue earning traffic had ceased some time before the line's actual official closure. Following complete closure, the station was used for a period commercially but now has been converted into holiday cottages as part of a caravan park.
Neville Stead Collection/Transport Treasury

On 7 August 1957 Class G5 No 67315 is seen in the platform at Thornton Dale with a freight heading towards Pickering. By this date, the branch was only open as far as Thornton Dale with the only traffic being stone from a local quarry. Constructed at Darlington as NER No 2086 in December 1900, the locomotive became No 7315 during August 1946. Having spent its BR career allocated to sheds in Tyneside and Northumberland, the locomotive was transferred to Malton in April 1956. This was destined to be its last reallocation, as it was withdrawn from Malton in December 1958. *Mike Mitchell/Transport Treasury*

Numerically the last of the Class J27 0-6-0s to be completed – at Darlington Works in September 1923 – No 65894 is seen at Kirbymoorside in 1964 shortly before the section from Gilling was closed completely. Kirbymoorside was the terminus of the line from 2 February 1953 when passenger services over the route were withdrawn and the line from Kirbymoorside to Pickering closed completely. The town the station served was actually called Kirkbymoorside, but the NER adopted the name 'Kirby Moorside' and the NER name survived through the LNER era until it was officially changed to 'Kirbymoorside' by BR on 31 May 1948. After the closure of the route to timetabled passenger services, the remaining section to Kirbymoorside was regularly used by excursion trains and other specials until 3 May 1964. The station buildings survived until being demolished in 2010; the site of the station is now occupied by a new housing development. No 65894 was allocated to York (North) between February 1950 and October 1966, when it was transferred to Sunderland. Withdrawn, after working the last diagrammed steam working from Sunderland, in September the following year – one of the last of the class to survive – the locomotive was preserved by the North Eastern Locomotive Preservation Group; the locomotive cost the group £1,400 (the equivalent of just over £26,000 at current prices). From October 1971 the locomotive has been based on the preserved North Yorkshire Moors Railway.
Neville Stead Collection/Transport Treasury

On 10 July 1964 the crossing keeper at Pockley Crossing, just to the east of Helmsley, closes the gates on the minor road that runs south from the A170. In a month's time – on 10 August – the job will become redundant with the final closure of the section from Gilling to Kirbymoorside. The labour-intensive nature of many of these rural railways undoubtedly affected their economics and, with the deterioration in BR's finances from the late 1950s onwards, their future was always going to be called into question. Although the crossing is no more, the substantial stone-built cottage provided for the crossing keeper is still extant.
Yorkshire Post/Transport Treasury

On 27 August 1959, Class J27 0-6-0 No 65844 is pictured departing from Helmsley with a short freight. By this date, the branch from Gilling only ran as far as Kirbymoorside. Helmsley was to retain its freight facilities until 10 August 1965. Helmsley station opened with the line on 9 October 1871 and was the largest on the branch; although Kirbymoorside handled more passengers, the busiest of the goods yards was that at Helmsley. Following closure, the station was converted into a private house. The substantial goods shed also survives with part of the yard in commercial use. The 'J27' was the last of three types of 0-6-0 built by the NER to the designs of William Worsdell; a total of 80 were built between 1906 and 1908 with a further 35 being completed between November 1921 and September 1923. The later locomotives were constructed to a slightly modified design by Vincent Raven that included superheating with slightly longer smokeboxes. All 115 passed to BR in 1948 with the last being withdrawn during 1967. One of the type – BR No 65894 – was preserved after withdrawal in September that year. No 65844 was one of the original batch; completed at Beyer Peacock in August 1908 as NER No 1211, it was to be renumbered 5844 as part of the LNER's 1946 renumbering scheme. When recorded here, the locomotive was allocated to Malton; it was transferred to York (North) in May 1963 from where it was withdrawn three months later. *Mike Mitchell/Transport Treasury*

The photographer grabbed a quick photograph of a York to Pickering via Helmsley service at Nunnington on 31 January 1953. The train was being hauled Class D49/1 No 62730 *Berkshire*. Designed by Sir Nigel Gresley, the first 36 locomotives – except for Nos 62726 and 62727 (which had been renamed by the LNER after modification) – of the type were named after shire counties and were all completed at Darlington Works between October 1927 and June 1929; No 62730 emerged in March 1929 and had originally been LNER No 2755 becoming No 2730 as part of the 1946 renumbering scheme. No 62730 was withdrawn in December 1958 and scrapped in may the following year; sister locomotive No 62712 *Morayshire* was preserved and is now part of the collection based on the Bo'ness & Kinneil Railway as LNER No 246. *Tony Wickens/Online Transport Archive*

On 5 August 1958 as a Class J27 0-6-0 heads in from the north with a short freight, the station at Nunnington has, by this date, lost its regular passenger services. Timetabled passenger services on the line from Pilmoor to Pickering were withdrawn on 2 February 1953 with the route closed completely between Kirbymoorside and Pickering from the same date. Excursion traffic from and to Nunnington continued, however, until 25 May 1963. The station retained its freight facilities until 10 August 1964 when the line was closed completely between Gilling and Kirbymoorside. The station at Nunnington remains intact having been converted into a private house.
Mike Mitchell/Transport Treasury

On 23 June 1957 the RCTS organised the 'Yorkshire Coast Rail Tour' from Leeds. The train traversed a number of lines including the section from Gilling to Kirbymoorside and return. Pictured taking water at Gilling during one of the train's two visits to the station is 'D49/1' 62731 *Selkirkshire*, which was one of four locomotives employed on the tour. By this date Gilling station was closed to passenger traffic but freight traffic continued until 10 August 1964. No 62731 was built as LNER No 2756 at Darlington Works in March 1929 and was renumbered 2731 in June 1946. When recorded here, the locomotive was allocated to York (North) shed but was to be transferred the next month to Selby from where it was withdrawn in April 1959. *Gavin Morrison*

On 27 May 1950 D49/2 No 62726 *The Meynell* is pictured awaiting departure from Gilling with an eastbound train. No 62726 was one of two of the original Class D49s – the other being No 62727 – which were fitted with Lenz rotary cam poppet valves in 1929 and became the precursors of the later 'Hunt' class D49/2s. The locomotives was completed, as LNER No 352 *Leicestershire*, at Darlington Works in March 1929 and was renamed in 1932. Renumbered 2726 in December 1946, when recorded here the locomotive was allocated to York (North) shed. It remained there until October 1953 when it was transferred to Scarborough, from where it was withdrawn in December 1957.
Tony Wickens/Online Transport Archive

On 10 August 1957 a member of the footplate crew keeps a wary eye on the photographer as 'V2' class 2-6-2 No 60906 eases its way gently across the level crossing at Coxwold with a westbound service towards Pilmoor. The level crossing was about half-a-mile west of the station and was controlled by a small crossing box as recorded here. The box was supervised by the box on the platform at Coxwold station and was interlocked with it. The box and gatekeeper's cottage are both still extant, having been converted into a private residence following the final closure of the line. The 'V2' was built at Darlington and completed in April 1940 as LNER No 4877; initially allocated the number 806 under the railway's first renumbering scheme of 1946, it was eventually to become No 906 in December of that year. Allocated to New England when recorded here, the locomotive had undergone a 63-day overhaul in Darlington Works between April and June 1957 and so was presumably on a running-in turn prior to being returned to its home depot. No 60906 was withdrawn from New England in May 1963. *Mike Mitchell/Transport Treasury*

Viewed from the 12-noon service from Darlington to Malton, this view records the signalbox at Coxwold on 30 August 1953. When the line through Coxwold opened, there was no passing loop between Gilling and Pilmoor; it was not until 1900 that the loop at Coxwold was opened. The original platform then became designated the down platform with the new one – with signalbox and platform shelter (visible in the distance) – being used for up trains. The box also controlled the sizeable goods yard at the station; freight facilities were withdrawn on 10 August 1965. Following closure to passenger services in 1953 the shelter visible was demolished.

Tony Wickens/Online Transport Archive

On 10 August 1957 BR Standard Class 5 No 73163, which had only been completed at Doncaster Works some six months earlier, heads west past the station at Husthwaite Gate with a service from Scarborough towards the East Coast main line. When the line opened on 1 June 1853 there was no station planned for the section between the East Coast main line and Coxwold. The origins of the station at Husthwaite Gate are uncertain but it first appeared in *Bradshaw* in February 1856. Initially nothing more than a simple platform was provided with basic freight facilities eventually being added. The wooden station building visible in this view was added in 1890; a goods shed was constructed at the same time. Regular timetabled passenger services ceased on 2 February 1953 although the line saw excursion traffic for the next decade. The station was closed completely with the withdrawal of freight facilities on 10 August 1964. The line west from Husthwaite Gate to Pilmoor had closed almost two years earlier, on 10 September 1962. Like many of the BR Standards, No 73163 was destined to have a very short operational life, being withdrawn in November 1965.

Mike Mitchell/Transport Treasury

The first station west of Battersby on the line towards Picton was Ingleby and photographed from the west Class G5 0-4-4T No 62788 is pictured arriving at the station with a service from Battersby. The station opened with the line on 3 March 1857. The section from Battersby to Picton was constructed with double track; however, as the ironstone traffic declined and with only a handful of passenger services – there were only two services per day from Battersby to Picton and three in the reverse direction during the summer of 1947, for example – during World War 2 the line became effectively single track, with all trains using the eastbound line. Thus, after having collected passengers at Ingleby, No 62788 will reverse its train over the crossover before heading west over the eastbound line. Passenger services between Battersby and Picton were withdrawn on 14 June 1965 with Ingleby station closing completely at the same time. The line between Stokesley, to the west of Ingleby, and Picton closed completely on 1 December 1958 and was lifted thereafter; the remaining section, from Battersby to Stokesley, closed on 2 August 1965. The station building, slightly modified, survives, having been rebuilt into a house.

Neville Stead Collection/Transport Treasury

In 1877 the NER opened a three-road brick-built engine shed at Battersby Junction. The shed, however, was destined to have a relatively short life accommodating locomotives as it closed in the early 1880s; reopened on 1 January 1889, it was again to close – this time permanently – on 30 November 1895. Thereafter the building had a number of uses, including the storage of redundant rolling stock, but by the date it was recorded here – 6 July 1952 – all track had been lifted. The building itself, however, was not finally to be demolished until 1965.
Tony Wickens/Online Transport Archive

On 3 May 1958 symmetry is seen at Battersby as Class A8 4-6-2T No 69877, in the Nunthorpe bay, and Class L1 2-6-4T No 67764 run round their respective trains. Passenger services west of Battersby to Picton had already been withdrawn by this date – on 14 June 1954 – and the route was closed completely between Picton and Stokesley on 1 December 1958; freight traffic continued west from Battersby to Stokesley until 2 August 1965. By May 1958, the 'A8' was approaching the end of its operational life – it was withdrawn in December 1959 – whilst the 'L1' was to survive until August 1962. *Tony Wickens/Online Transport Archive*

On 5 July 1965, the driver of Type 3 (later Class 37) No D6778 has both the road and the single-line token as the freight departs from Battersby station. Note the disconnected loop in the Nunthorpe bay platform. By this date the section west from Battersby, open only as far as Stokesley by this date, was approaching its last few days; it was to close on 2 August 1965. No D6778 was built by Robert Stephenson & Hawthorn Ltd and entered service in October 1962. Based at Thornaby when new, it remained allocated there until October 1971 when it moved to March. Renumbered 37.078 under the TOPS scheme in February 1974, it was finally withdrawn in January 2004 after more than 40 years' service. Originally known as Ingleby Junction when opened on 1 April 1868, the station became Battersby Junction on 30 September 1878 and simply Battersby from 1 May 1893.
Henry Priestley/Transport Treasury

The NER opened a two-road engine shed close to the terminus of the West Rosedale branch on 27 March 1961. The shed was extended in 1862. The mines that locomotives allocated to the shed closed in 1925 but traffic continued for a brief period until 1929 as calcine dust was extracted from the slag heaps. Following the cessation of this traffic, the last locomotive allocated to the shed was transferred away on 8 June 1929. In order to lower it via the 1 in 5 gradient of the Ingleby incline, the centre wheels had to be removed. The shed was closed thereafter; in 1937 the building was demolished with the stone being used in the construction of the village hall in Hutton-le-Hole. This is the site of the demolished shed, taken from the north, on 6 July 1952. The surviving stonework gives an indication of the substantial structure that it once was. *Tony Wickens/Online Transport Archive*

Although the railway line from Battersby to Grosmont was completed during the 1860s, there was no provision for a station at Commondale – viewed here from the east – although a siding was installed for the Cleveland Fire Brick & Pottery Co. This enterprise resulted in an increase in the local population and, from Bradshaw in December 1882 (when the name first appeared), 'Commondale Siding' was shown. It was not until 1891, however, that the station illustrated here was completed when the stop became simply 'Commondale'. Passenger traffic was never great and, from 16 January 1950, the station became an unstaffed halt – the first on the line – and it remains open serving trains between Whitby and Middlesbrough. *Henry Priestley/Transport Treasury*

An eastbound DMU is pictured standing in the single platform at Danby. Although undated, the photograph predates 2 August 1965 as there is evidence of some freight traffic in the small goods yard to the north of the station. Danby station opened with the line from Castleton Moor to Grosmont on 2 October 1865; although the line had originally been promoted by the North Yorkshire & Cleveland Railway, by the time that the route opened the original company had been incorporated into the NER and it was the larger company that completed the construction of the Esk Valley line. *Henry Priestley/Transport Treasury*

Pictured from the east, this view of Lealholm station records the location after the removal of the passing loop. The line through Lealholm – promoted by the North Yorkshire & Cleveland Railway – opened between Castleton Moor and Grosmont on 2 October 1865 with Lealholm station opening at the same time. The NER referred to the station as 'Lealholme' or 'Lealholm Bridge' in timetables at various times. The station, with its associated goods shed, was built by the contractor Thomas Nelson. Freight facilities were withdrawn from Lealholm on 2 August 1965 but the station remains open for services to and from Whitby. Today, the stone-built station and goods shed remain, as does the disused up platform, although the small signalbox visible on the platform has been demolished.

Henry Priestley/Transport Treasury

On 15 August 1961 Class J27 No 65844 is pictured approaching Scarborough Road Junction, in Malton, with the return pick-up freight from the Gilling branch. Freight traffic on the section from Husthwaite Gate to Amotherby ceased on 10 August 1964 simultaneously with the final closure of the section from Gilling to Kirbymoorside. The short remaining section from Amotherby to Malton East and the link from Malton East to Scarborough Road Junction closed completely on 19 October 1964. The route to Amotherby survived for slightly longer than the rest of the route as a result of a contract with the Brandsbys Agricultural Trading Association. The line beyond Malton East to Driffield had closed completely on 20 October 1958. The signalbox at Scarborough Road Junction was abolished with the final closure of the branch and was subsequently demolished. No 65844 was completed as NER No 1211 by Beyer Peacock in August 1908; renumbered 5844 in March 1946 as part of the LNER renumbering scheme, when recorded here the locomotive was appropriately allocated to Malton shed. It was transferred to York (North) in May 1963, from where it was withdrawn three months later.
Mike Mitchell/Transport Treasury